# Herb Gardening For Beginners:

# Essential Tips on How to Plant and Grow Herbs in Herb Garden

By

Erin Morrow

# Table of Contents

Introduction .......................................................................... 5

Chapter 1. Top Ten Benefits of Herb Gardening................... 6

Chapter 2. Materials For Growing a Herb Garden ................ 9

Chapter 3. Herbs That Are Great For Planting and Cooking 11

Chapter 4. Five Steps to Growing Herbs From Seeds ......... 13

Chapter 5. Ten Steps For Beginning a Herb Garden ........... 16

Chapter 6. Planting and Harvesting ..................................... 22

Chapter 7. Five Tips For a Successful First Herb Garden .... 24

Chapter 8. Common Mistakes ............................................. 26

Chapter 9. Herb Gardening Indoors..................................... 29

Conclusion ........................................................................... 32

Thank You Page ................................................................... 33

Herb Gardening For Beginners: Essential Tips on How to Plant and Grow Herbs in Herb Garden

By Erin Morrow

© Copyright 2015 Erin Morrow

Reproduction or translation of any part of this work beyond that permitted by section 107 or 108 of the 1976 United States Copyright Act without permission of the copyright owner is unlawful. Requests for permission or further information should be addressed to the author.

This publication is designed to provide accurate and authoritative information in regard to the subject matter covered. This work is sold with the understanding that the publisher is not engaged in rendering legal, accounting, or other professional services. If legal advice or other expert assistance is required, the services of a competent professional person should be sought.

First Published, 2015

Printed in the United States of America

# Introduction

Are you a chef or a cook that enjoys using different types of herbs in your cooking? Wouldn't you like to have your own herbs in abundance and always have a stash available every time you are in the kitchen? You can create your own herb garden, now is the time to consider having one in your backyard. If you are a beginner you may be uncertain as to when to start planting, well you can get started during the spring. Working your herb garden will take you all the way through the summer.

Herb gardens do require some extra work and if you have patience you will be successful. Herbs grow really well with some sunlight exposure, soil that has good water drainage, fertilizing and mulching. Herbs can grow in pots, containers and plant-beds. However, according to experts, herb gardening flourishes best in the ground as they are known to spread. Certain herb plants can grow between 4 to 6 feet. As seeds they are placed in containers and pots, they are often transplanted during their developmental stage.

# Chapter 1. Top Ten Benefits of Herb Gardening

Maybe you are wondering why you should take all this extra time and grow herbs when you can just go to the supermarket. The following are ten benefits to growing your own herb garden.

1. Always Available Fresh Herbs – The number one benefit to growing your own herbs is that you will always have them fresh whenever you need them. It can be inside or outside but you will never have to leave your house for them.

2. Say Goodbye to Boring Dinners – Cooking with herbs will make your plan old dish turn into a brand new meal. The possibilities are endless, your only limit is the number of herbs you plant.

3. They are Good for You – Adding herbs to your regular diet will increase the vitamin content of your meal. Plus, gardening is great exercise. After a couple weeks of digging, stretching and bending you will begin to see some toned muscles.

4. Money Saver – Buying fresh herbs at the supermarket can be expensive. Plus, they don't always have what you are looking for. Once you pay for the initial start-up of your garden, you will be saving money on all your herbs.

5. Herbs are Educational – Gardening can be an educational experience for both adults and children. There is always something that can be learned. For example, recipes, techniques, new uses and the history of the herbs.

6. Stress Relieve – Horticulture therapy is a much accepted practice in the world today. Plus, the smell and the beautiful sight of a herbal garden can ignite your senses and make you feel new.

7. Curb Appeal – When you add a garden to your landscape it gives your home more curb appeal. Herbs are as lovely as many shrubs and flowers.

8. Sharing – When you grow your own herbs, you will likely have more than you need for person use. You can share with your neighbors, family and friends.

9. Extensive Variety – There are so many different types of herbs. Take basil for example, there are over

30 types. When you grow your own herb garden you will get to taste the different varieties that are often not sold in stores.

10. It is Fun – Gardening isn't the cleanest activity but it is fun and offers a sense of satisfaction. When you grow your own herb garden you will have fun and inherit a world of benefits.

## Chapter 2. Materials For Growing a Herb Garden

Growing herbs from seeds will mean that you need added materials to generate a successful garden. It is important to invest in a few materials for the success of your garden.

- You will need a medium sized bag to grow your herb seeds. At this point don't use garden soil as it may not be nutritious for the development of the seeds.

- You may need different kinds of seed trays that have divided sections and translucent plastic covers. You can start by purchasing the Seed Starter Kit that can be found on Amazon for very cheap. The cover on this starter kit protects the seeds as well as maintaining the dampness of the soil during the time of germination. If you intend on growing several kinds of herbs you will need around 3 or 4 of these starter kits. If you are only starting with one type of herb just purchase one.

- You will need a garden strainer. The garden sieve is vital for straining compost and covering your seeds after you have planted them.

- Water spraying device. You will need a water sprayer or small watering can with a detachable device that has small holes that will water the seeds gently and not move them from their positions. The goal is to get your herbs to develop and formed roots, so that it will be ready for transplanting later on.

- Sufficient plastic herb containers or pots. You will need to have enough of the right sized pots or containers. These are needed to house the herb seeds in which you will be planting.

Other helpful gardening tools include; gardening gloves, kneeling cushion, hoe, rake, pruners, a hori hori (for cutting weeds), an ergonomic shovel, an easy bloom plant sensor (detects sunlight and moisture in the area), a gardening apron, compost tumbler, a cobra head (for weeding), and a journal to keep notes on your growing process.

## Chapter 3. Herbs That Are Great For Planting and Cooking

There are a vast range of herbs that you can plant in your first herb garden. Remember choose herbs that will grow well in the environment you have available. Also, it is okay to start small and add more plants later. It is better to under plant than overplant. Here is a list of some of the best herbs to grow in your garden for eating.

- Basil: These offer a warm and spicy flavor. Great for soups, salads, omelettes, pesto, and meats.

- Chives: These herbs have a mild onion flavor. They are great when chopped up and used in cheese dishes.

- Coriander: The young leaves of this herb are called cilantro. They are great in soups and with avocado.

- Dill: These fresh leaves can be used to season soups, meats, salad and potatoes.

- Fennel: The leaves are sweet. They tend to be used a lot for sauces, fish, veal and pork.

- Mint: These leaves are great for brewing in tea, sprinkling over lamp or used in sauces or jams.

These are just a few of the herbs that you can try. Parsley and sage are two other great choices. Find the herb that is right for your family and garden.

## Chapter 4. Five Steps to Growing Herbs From Seeds

Following these instructions will help you generate a healthy and successful herb garden.

Step 1 – After having bought your trays fill them with soil-less humus. Utilize a water sprayer or watering can with a detachable device with fine holes to water the seed trays. Do not soak the seed trays. Then place 2 to 3 seeds in each of the divided sections of the tray

Step 2 – Gently cover the seed containers with finely strained non-soil compost. It is recommended to not deeply bury the seeds. Then gently spray the containers with water again and cover them with the plastic covers. It is advised, to label your trays so that you know which container has which kind of herb, especially if you planted several different types of herbs.

Step 3 – It is recommended that you cover the containers with newspaper and place them in a green house on a platform. Place them where you can reach them without feeling any back aches or pains when bending over. Pay close attention to your herb seeds on a daily basis and keep the moisture level of the compost balanced. Constantly check the germination process of the herb seeds.

Step 4 – After the seeds have germinated remove the newspaper layer from the seed containers. Then place the trays or containers in an area where they will receive a balance of shade and some mild sunlight.

Step 5 – Transplant the seedlings from the compartmentalized trays or containers into plastic pots with nutritious compost. After the herbs are about 2 to 3 inches in height, place them in the pots that are filled with 3 to 4 inches of soil-less compost. Be sure that the pots have a hole in the middle for water drainage. Remember when you transfer the young plants move them carefully and gently holding them by the mass formed by the roots of the plant to avoid losing any roots. After you have placed every herb in a pot make sure that the compost around is firm so that it can support the herb plant. Keep the herb plants in a fresh and cool area like a greenhouse and water them daily. Water them very early in the morning or late in the evening. After the plants have grown taller and stronger they are ready to be transplanted into the garden area that you have been preparing.

## Chapter 5. Ten Steps For Beginning a Herb Garden

If you have never planted an herb garden, you will need some direction. Follow these ten steps and you will be off to a great start.

Step 1. Devise a Plan. If you fail to plan great ideas for your garden, most likely your future garden will be a failure. You want to get started on the right foot. Sketch out your plan, write down everything you will need, do your research and gather information on herb gardening for beginners. If you are not satisfied with the data you collected, visit your nearest garden center and talk to the experts on herb gardening. Remember, if you have a list of everything you will need and what you want to plant then you are on the right track. Start small and as you go, if you feel inspired, continue, and you can expand your territory. The main idea is to enjoy what you will be doing from the beginning to the end.

Step 2. Choose where you will be planting. Almost every plant requires around 6 hours of sunlight every day. It doesn't matter if it takes you more than a day to choose your spot. When choosing the area where you will be planting study the movements of the sun along with the areas that may have lots of trees. Ask yourself, "Is the area you are going to choose sunny enough for your herbs?" Additionally, a good idea when you purchase your herb seeds is to check the packets for the amount of sunlight recommended or ask the garden specialists at your nearest garden center.

The location of the garden is just as important as how much sunlight it will require. The closer the garden it is to you, the quicker you can have access to it in terms of maintaining it and keeping watch over it.

Step 3. Clean out the area. Before planting your herbs you may want to clean out the area where you will be planting. Remove the sod and for more efficient results, till the ground. Others recommend you smother the ground with newspaper and then leave the newspaper on for a few days to choke away any remaining weeds. A layer of five sheets is thick enough. The goal of this step is to rid your garden of any weeds and pests so that you can have healthy herbs growing in your garden area.

Step 4. Enrich the soil. Soil that will be used for planting herbs needs to be revitalized. As the nutrients in the soil are not enough for the whole planting season. To give the soil a boost you can blend some organic substances, add compost (2 to 3 inch layers). In your compost you should include; manure, dry grass cuttings, decomposed leaves and small shredded sticks. Then till the soil and mix all the organic substances in the soil until the soil becomes loose.

If you use an alternate approach like plant beds for your herbs then you are unable to dig, simply leave the compost on the surface and watch how it will penetrate through the soil within a few months. If you are planting your herbs in containers or pots, simply combine a mixture of compost with organic matter, then sieve it and then fill the pots and containers with it.

Step 5. Till your soil before planting. This step focuses on what happens when you till the soil. Ploughing the soil loosens it. When the soil is loose the roots of the herb plants are able to infiltrate the soil rather easily. Note-well, digging the ground when it is too dry or too wet can ruin its formation. The right time to dig the soil is when it has moisture. The best way to tell if the soil is right is to hold the soil in your hand and make it into the shape of a ball (it should hold together loosely) and when you put it back down it will fall apart. When digging the soil use a pitch fork and dig about 8 to 12 inches deep, blending the compost as you go along as mentioned during Step 4.

Step 6. Select your plants. Well in this case we obviously know what we want to plant. Go to the nearest garden center and buy what interests you. Select herbs that will grow well in your climates, soil and sunlight.

Step 7. Plant the herbs in the ground. Planting herbs in the ground is an excellent choice as they develop much faster and grow larger when they have ample room. When planting them in the ground check with your nearest garden expert for tips. Learn the right dates, times and seasons. Mid-spring and mid-autumn are the way to go. You can even be successful all through the summer since the soil will not be too cold or wet.

Step 8. Water Herbs Sufficiently. Water herbs gently especially when they are just seeds. They should be watered enough so they remain moist so as to survive throughout the day. If you overwater the herbs while at the seed stage they will simply rotten out. Always pay close attention to the herb on a daily basis.

If you planted the herbs in containers and then transplanted them make sure you water the herb plants frequently so their roots attach firmly into the soil. After having transplanted the herbs the amount of watering will depend on the moisture of the soil with the mixture of compost, the humidity of the weather and how frequently it rains. When it is hot and dry, herb plants will demand more water. When watering the herbs, take your time and allow the water to penetrate deeply into the soil and roots to soak them sufficiently. The best time to water the herb plants is very early in the morning and late evening. Watering the herb seeds or plants midday especially when the sun is hot may scorch them.

Step 9. Mulching. Mulching eliminates weeds and absorbs water. This keeps the herbs nutritiously growing. Add a layer of 2 to 3 inches of mulch on top of the soil.

Step 10. Be consistent and Persistent. Planting your herb garden as a first timer may not be a simple task.

You will need to be willing to get your hands dirty as well as have much patience. Your herbs will need to be watered consistently, weeds will need to be pulled frequently, and mulching will need to be done seasonally.

# Chapter 6. Planting and Harvesting

**Planting Herbs**

One of the main things to consider when growing plants is making sure they are in the right location. Most herbs do best in full sun, with temperatures under 90 degrees. If it gets hotter than that, you can put them in an area that has sun in the morning but a bit of shade in the afternoon.

You will need about 1 to 4 feet in diameter for each plant. Here are some suggestions for common herb plants:

- Rosemary, Mints, Sage, Marjoram and Oregano need 3 to 4 feet.

- Thyme, Savory, Basils and Tarragon need 2 feet.

- Cilantro, Dill, Chives and Parsley need 1 foot.

**Harvesting your Herbs**

If its harvest time for your herbs all you need to do is cut 1/3 of the branches, when the plant reaches 6 to 8 feet tall. When you cut close to the leaves intersection your plants will regrow quickly. Some plants, like parsley, have new leaves that grow from the center. If this is the case for your herbs then you need to remove the oldest branches first. The more time you spend with your plants you will begin to see how they grow.

# Chapter 7. Five Tips For a Successful First Herb Garden

The following are some great tips and tricks for the first time planter. If you follow these you are surely going to be successful.

Tip #1 – When planting your first garden consider the climate in your region. If it is too sunny and it gets really hot throughout the summer cover the herbs with layers of 2 or 3 inches of compost. This will maintain a certain level of moisture and will keep your herbs growing healthy.

Tip #2 – Get information on the height and width of each herb. Place them in sequence of height starting from the shortest to the tallest herbs that way you can have easy access to them in your garden.

Tip #3 – Give each herb its required space and pay attention to how each one grows. For example, Creeping Thyme versus Regular Thyme, each grow differently. Creeping Thyme also has a different reaction while growing and it needs to be controlled so that it does not hamper with other herbs.

Tip #4 – Label each and every one of the herb plants so you know which is which. A number of plants look similar and while you are harvesting it is best to know which is which.

Tip #5 – Maintain a consistent and persistent enthusiasm and nourish your garden daily. This will help you to reap a successful herb garden for the long run.

## Chapter 8. Common Mistakes

Herb gardening can seem like a challenging undertaking but it is really not all that different than other types of gardening. If you follow all the steps and watch out for common mistakes you are sure to be successful. The following are ten common mistakes that people make with herb gardens and how to avoid them.

Mistake #1 – Selecting Unhealthy Herb Plants: You want plants that are healthy, have a bright color, and lots of foliage. There should be no sign of bugs or eggs. If you see one bug, you can be certain there are more. Do not feel bad for the scrawny herb. Look for the healthiest herbs available.

Mistake #2 – Planting in the Wrong Places: You need to plant the herbs where they belong. If you are planting something like rosemary and it likes dry soil, it has no business being in a damp and humid environment. Planting herbs that need sun will wilt if they are in the shade. Find a way to put your herbs into the right environments.

Mistake #3 – Not Pruning Enough: Rapid growth comes from good pruning. Failure to prune will lead to a lack of growth and leaves drying up. When you harvest regularly you keep the herb growing and producing for longer. Plus, your herbs look better when pruned regularly.

Mistake #4 – Overcrowding: It is important to make note of the full height and width of a full grown plant. Often times people try and grow too much in one space, it is always better to under plant than overplant.

Mistake #5 – Letting your Flowers turn to Seeds: When herb plants begin to flower, it is a mark of the end of their lifespan. When you see a flower beginning to form it is best to remove the flower.

Mistake #6 – Spraying Chemicals: Do not use chemicals for insect control on your herb garden. Herbs should never have contact with chemicals, it can be toxic to those who consume it. You can avoid chemicals by taking preventative measures. These include; weeding regularly, watch for insects, and fertilize naturally.

Mistake #7 – Forgetting the Small Details: Keep a close eye on your herbs. Watch for damaged ground, disturbed soil, and damaged leaves. If you detect a problem early enough you may be able to correct it.

Mistake #8 – Not Watering Correctly: Herbs need a water schedule maintained. Aim to water them in the morning, water will soak further into the soil and evaporation will be avoided. Do not water the leaves. The right mulch is also a great plan for herbs, it keeps the soil moist.

Mistake #9 – Not Protecting your Herbs: Herbs tend to be resistant to bugs and disease but it still happens. While you should not use chemicals, there are some organic ways for you to control insect problems.

Mistake #10 – Not Fertilizing: All-purpose fertilizer will help keep your plant growing nicely. Compost tea about once a week will give them a health boost. When you compost be sure to avoid the leaves.

Everyone makes mistakes. If you make a mistake with your herb garden, learn from it and try again. After learning is one of the benefits of herb gardening anyway.

## Chapter 9. Herb Gardening Indoors

If you don't have the time or space to grow an herb garden outdoors, you can start one indoors. It is much simpler to grow herbs than most houseplants. All you will need is large containers and a warm and sunny environment. A benefit to growing your herbs in containers, is that you never have to go through the hassle of getting a large garden started. However, if you do have the time and space plants are always better off in the ground. If you are planning on growing herbs indoors in a container, they will need regular water and light.

Below is a list of the necessities:

- Large Containers – Either made from plastic or clay. They should be between 8 and 18 inches in diameter.

- Good Soil – You should have enough soil to fill your pots.

- Plant Fertilizer – Vegetable or Organic is recommended.

- Hose or Watering Can – Inside Herbs need to be watered regularly.

These are the steps you should follow for a successful indoor herb garden:

Step #1 – Prepare your Container: Fill it with soil and add fertilizer in accordance with the directions.

Step #2 – Ready the Soil: Make sure your soil is damp. Mix water until the moisture is all the way through.

Step #3 – Protect your Deck or Counter: Place your pot on its saucer.

Step #4 – Dig Holes: Your holes should be big enough for each plant.

Step #5 – Transfer your Herbs: Remove the Herb from its starter container. Turn it over, tap the bottom and pull gently at the stem base until the plant comes out. Then put your Herbs into their new home, fill in soil around the edges.

Step #6 – Watering: Water your new herb plant immediately after planted. Only water when the soil is dry.

If you follow these step by step instructions you will have a flourishing indoor garden. Make sure your herbs get at least four hours of sun each day or they will not grow well.

## Conclusion

Creating an herb garden in your yard, is an opportunity to experience many benefits. Herb Gardening has a number of benefits including; saving money, always having fresh herbs, a larger variety and much more. If you follow the instructions, watch out for mistakes and pay good attention to your garden, you will be harvesting great herbs throughout the growing season.

Get started with your herb garden today, but make sure you choose the best herbs, place them in the best locations for their growth and water them regularly. Before you know it you will be sharing herbs with your friends, family and neighbors.

## Thank You Page

I want to personally thank you for reading my book. I hope you found information in this book useful and I would be very grateful if you could leave your honest review about this book. I certainly want to thank you in advance for doing this.

If you have the time, you can check my other books too.

www.ingramcontent.com/pod-product-compliance
Lightning Source LLC
LaVergne TN
LVHW021745060526
838200LV00052B/3482